PAIN IN MY HEART

DARYL-JAROD

Daryl-Jarod Entertainment
www.daryljarod.com

Manufactured in the United States of America

Cover Photography by Hallo Smith
Cover Design by Kelly Thomas

First Trade Paperback Edition November 2019

ISBN: 978-1-945748-13-4 (pbk)
ISBN: 978-1-945748-12-7 (ebook)

For Rashaunda…
Who taught me I should always be true to myself. And within that, lies true happiness.

Heavenly Father, thank you so much for breath in my lungs and the opportunity to release yet another book. The blessings continue flowing!

Hallo Smith, I must say any and all of my expectations have been exceeded with the photography, as always! It's rare I run across another artist who can interpret my vision and take it to another level. Thank you, thank you, thank you!!!

Kelly Thomas, your friendship means the world to me! Thank you for putting up with me and my indecisiveness. Your graphic design skills are incredible and I can't wait for our next project!

Readers, thank you for taking a chance on this book. I appreciate each and every one of you. And I hope you enjoy!

TABLE OF CONTENTS

~PART ONE~
"Happiness is a state of mind
Not everyone is so lucky to find"

~PART TWO~
"It's so cold
In this lonely heart of mine"

~PART THREE~
"A promise is nothing more than a lie
A lie waiting to be broken"

~PART FOUR~
"Internally bleeding on the inside
Faking a smile on the outside"

~PART FIVE~
*"You're a liability
I can't risk falling for"*

~PART SIX~
"...He exhaled"

*"Happiness is a state of mind
Not everyone is so lucky to find"*

NO TURNING BACK

Knife to his throat

Pain in his heart

He contemplates his life

And realizes there's no turning back

If he takes this leap

He could surely change his fate

But if he gives up now

What about those he'll leave behind?

Is it selfish to want the nagging pain to end?

Is it absurd to wish those tears away?

Is it truly a sin to play God

And end your own life?

I WONDER

I wonder, would they miss me?

If one day I decided I'd grown tired of trying

And wanted nothing more

To do with this *cruel, cruel* world

If I woke up one morning too weary

Of being called sissy and faggot

Too ashamed of living day-to-day in this skin

Because no one seems to understand me

They have no interest at all

In comprehending my daily struggles

Just because I walk the way I walk

And talk the way I talk

Does that give anyone the right to exclude me?

Or find humor in my uniqueness?

Is it even ethical to taunt a timid soul

Already on the brink of destruction?

If I suddenly decided to give into

The darkness that follows

And if I for once and for all

No longer had to endure the torment

Of bullies and insecure bystanders

Would anyone care?

Tell me, would anyone care at all?

I wonder…

BLACK DEMON

He remains dark and sinister

Blocking even the smallest trace of light

Trailing behind in the shadows

As his cruel intentions remain clear

At any given moment

He's ready to take this precious life

Terrified of giving in

To what he craves more and more each day

I fall down to my knees

And pray he'd simply go away

For him to leave me be

For him to give me peace

For him to set me

FREE!

*"It's so cold
In this lonely heart of mine
I need warmth
From a soul
That speaks to mine"*

CUPID DONE SHOT ME DOWN

All alone in the world

Without a love to call my own

I find myself losing hope

Of finding a love worth fighting for

But just in the nick of time

Just when I predicted I'd never fall again

Cupid swooped down

And changed my fate

I'm positive all the lovers out there can relate

And surely attest to the fact that

When the arrow pierces through your heart

It's not up for debate

You've been chosen

For two souls to intertwine

Let go of all the hurt inside

And allow their hearts to cross that finish line

ANOTHER HIT

I think I need another hit

But it's not just the drugs that captivate

My soul when I stare into those dark brown eyes

It's that clever mind

That keeps my head spinning

Lips smiling

And love below pulsating

Wondering what would happen if we ever

Joined forces and became ONE

If we allowed our withheld thoughts

To escape through our lips

And outline an entirely new destiny

Maybe it's all just from the high

But just one touch and I'm on cloud nine

And as long as I'm next to you

I could care less about coming down

Could we put that lighter to ya blunt

And spark up another?

I'm damn near dying

To see how far we'd go with another

MY MUSE

My muse

My inspiration

My drive to succeed

My undeniably fascinating motivation

In the wee hours of the night

I lie in bed silently thanking you

In the back of my mind

I remain forever grateful

A muse like you could never be duplicated

Never ever dissipated

Cuz you seem to

Forever have my mind simulated

Forever your vessel to be illuminated

...SEARCHING

We're all in need of that

Knock us off our feet kinda lovin'

The kind of love to break the curse

Of failed relationships and wasting our time

The rare type of love

To bypass the negativity and bullshit

The kind that won't hesitate

To love us back in return

The Rare type
of Love.

DON'T LET GO

I desperately want this feeling to last forever

Because when I look into your eyes

I catch a glimpse of your soul

A soul so pure, yet fragile

You seem so well put together on the outside

But I see all the broken pieces

I hope to put together again

You desperately attempt to hide from the world

Only because you've been hurt so many times

So have I…

Giving a portion of yourself to those unworthy

Has you afraid to let me inside

And mend what he destroyed

Still I close my eyes and pray to the heavens

You'll see I'm one in a million

That you'll let down your guard

To realize I'm nothing like the rest

It's as simple as opening your eyes

And allowing yourself to what's in front of you
Before it's too late

I'm stretching out my arms to you
Crying out for you to grab ahold
And love me like I know you can

Don't let go of me love
Don't let go

THE JOY OF FALLING IN LOVE

Hearts beating so loudly through our clothes

That we can faintly hear it outside our chests

He stares at me and sees his future

I pray this moment lasts forever

THE LOVE BELOW

Waking me up like a hot cup of Folgers

Spreading your love deep within me

Until my cup overflows

This is how I like it

Witnessing that look in your eyes

As your love below expands

And moves with precision

Both of us panting and weeping

Pushing our bodies to insanity

Bringing us both to that point of no return

Where lust transcends to the unimaginable

And those three words

Rest on the tip of our tongues

STRUNG OUT

When his love roamed inside of me

I could've sworn he touched my soul

It was gentle enough

For me to handle with ease

Yet heavy enough

To leave me begging for more

SOUL DEEP

Can you go so deep you touch my soul?

So deep I forget the pain?

So deep I tap out from the pleasure of you?

TEARS UPON MY PILLOW

These tears upon my pillow confirm it all

I've fallen for you

Threw caution to the wind

With no safety net to catch me at all

*"A promise is nothing more than a lie
A lie waiting to be broken"*

THE TRUTH ABOUT LOVE

The truth about love is...

It tricks you into letting go

And giving your energy

To someone you envision

Spending the rest of your days with

It boasts about being patient

But turns around only to disappoint

Claiming it's true and kind

Yet still splitting out lies

The truth about love is...

It builds you up with promises

Then leaves you high and dry

HATE

They say hate is such a strong word
But what can I say except I hate you
I really fucking hate you

Lord forgive these evil thoughts
Take away the burden from this heavy heart
It's difficult reaching for the light
When the devil's got a hold of you

What other word is there to describe you?
Within the pages of a Webster dictionary
There lies your name, LUCIFER
In bold red ink

Who else but the devil would find pleasure
In playing sick, twisted games
On an innocent soul?
Who else but a bastard would embarrass me
Just to leave me in the cold?

Who else but YOU would toss away the glove

And attempt to infect me with poison?

Yes, hate is a strong word

And I seriously fucking hate you

NO

The word "no"

Is defined as meaning refusal or disapproval

It's used to express one's human right

To stand up for themselves

And reject anything he/she may not desire

Mankind knows this

We all know this

But you said the word "no" does not exist

Nope

It doesn't exist when it comes to you

You could demand I climb the highest mountain

And then instruct me to jump

All while convinced I'd do it

Because you said I could never say no

That's why all those years ago

On the third floor, in my own bedroom

I remained mute, body flinched

As you did what you pleased

All because you said

Never say no

LIVING NIGHTMARE

I'm afraid to close my eyes at night

Because there you are once again

Haunting my dreams

Violating my thoughts

Stealing all of my peace

LIKE YOU NEVER EXISTED

Yesterday I scrolled through my phone

Grimaced at your contact info

Then proceeded to delete everything

Every text, every photo, every missed call

Everything that reminded me of you

But I didn't stop there

Oh no, oh no

I went even further

Not long after I disposed of all your belongings

Your clothes, everything you gave me

Every single possession associated with you

Why?

Because who needs memories

When they hurt you even more?

Who needs to be constantly reminded

Of pain and all the petty shit you did?

Why should I waste another moment
Thinking of what used to be
When we're both well aware
I've rarely crossed your mind?

From there, I went one step further
And I erased you from my heart
Matter of fact
I locked up this failing heart
Placed chains on the door
And buried the key six feet deep

Forever gone are the memories
Forever gone are the harsh reminders
I'm moving on and pressing forward
Like you never even existed

HEARTBREAK 101

The naïve need not apply

Anyone who believes in true love

Should keep themselves at bay

Cuz this heartbreak right here

…This shit is for the birds

BROKEN PIECES

He stole a piece of my soul

The day he left me high and dry

He dimmed the brightness of my light

When he left me in the bone-chilling cold

He didn't care then

Doesn't faze him now

As I'm left to pick up the pieces

Of a fragile broken heart

NEVER AGAIN

I'll never love as hard

As I used to love

I'll never kiss as passionately

As I used to kiss

I'll never trust the way

I used to trust

I'll never fall so hard

Because with love

There's no safety net

LOVE?

He didn't have to say he loved me

But he did

He confessed his love for me

Boasted it was a far deeper love

Than all the others

Even claimed he'd

Travel through hell and high water

Swim the deepest sea

Just to prove

He loved me

And only me

WHERE DID HE GO?

But where is he now?

Why did he disappear

Once the honeymoon phase

Passed us by?

Why isn't he here

To kiss away my fallen tears?

MISERY LOVES COMPANY

It baffles me

How much bullshit

You'll put up with

When you're lonely

LUV IS BLIND

Goodness grief!

It happened again

I fell in love

With the wrong one

Eyes wide open

But still blinded at the same time

LIAR, LIAR

They'll all lead you to believe

They sincerely have your

Best intentions at heart

And yet they still disappoint

THE HEART WANTS WHAT THE HEART WANTS

He warned me not to love him

He wasn't prepared for it

Wasn't accustomed to it

Honestly couldn't handle it

Did I listen?

Do I ever?

"Internally bleeding on the inside
Faking a smile on the outside"

PAIN IN MY HEART

It's this agonizing pain in my heart
That makes me fear I'll never love again
I've always been such a romantic
A hopeless romantic
Always willing and ready to love

It's this gut-piercing pain in my heart
That allows the bitterness to overtake me
Losing out on sleep
Wondering about any and everything
He's doing with my replacement

It's this soul-drenching pain in my heart
That's now too afraid to let love in
Too burnt out from fear and worry
Of what pain the next man
Might bring onto this barely beating heart

THE AFTERMATH

Scars so deep

They'll never ever heal

Shortness of breath

And vitals pretty low

All are nothing more

Than aftermath of what you did to me

THE AFTERMATH PT. 2

He said he loved me

But all this time

He told me what I needed to hear

All while loving someone else

THE AFTERMATH PT. 3

I fucked up…

Closed my eyes

And dreamed of you

…again

Except this time

You actually wanted me

Just as much as I want you

NUMB

Just need one more shot

To chase the pain away

Give me one more dose

To keep the dreams at bay

And I continue sipping the night away

Until I feel nothing at all

Not a single tear, not one worry

From here your face fades away

But the emptiness remains

DAMN THIS LONELINESS

Loneliness got the best of me

Double texted you after no response

Sat and waited for a reply that never came

Cursed myself for every attempt to feel wanted

TICK TOCK

12 am

I popped a bottle

And told myself you were simply busy

1am

I poured a second glass

With hopes you'd hit me up by the third

2am

I finished the bottle

And pondered on throwing out your clothes

3am

I cried

While telling myself

Right here ain't where you wanna be

WHAT ABOUT ME?

He only touches me when he needs release

All my needs appear to be obsolete

MY ONLY REGRET

I wish I could unfuck you

Then maybe I wouldn't care as much

Wasting so much energy on someone

Who never gave a fuck from the start

BODY COUNT

Body count rises
Self-esteem lowers

I opened up my walls to you
To help me forget

You opened up your home to me
Cuz you needed a fix

And now that the deed is done
I'll never see your face again

Now that we both have cum
I'm not the least bit attracted to you

We repeat this cycle over and over
Searching for a void we'll never really fill

Body count rises
Self-esteem lowers

BODY

I gave him the nickname "Body"

Cuz although we had nothing in common

He was there to keep me warm at night

He kept the nightmares at bay

Yet a tad bit selfish

And maybe a bit too needy

I ignored it all

All because that body shielded me from the cold

For all we really need

Is someone who will help us feel safe

Even if it's merely a warm canvas

In the wee hours of the night

FUCK BOYS

No matter how much I try

No matter how hard I love

I always end up with these fuck boys

These aggy, no good for nothing...fuck boys

They drain my energy

And suck the life out of me

Fill my head with broken promises

We both know won't come true

Beg for my body with no intentions

Of loving my mind

And when the answer is no

They vanish like a thief in the night

No longer wanting to deal with the BS

No longer opening doors to my wounded heart

I still end up with these fuck boys

These lying, no good for nothing...fuck boys

I could tell them I'm tired of the games

Tell them only the serious need to apply

For a chance at my love

Should only be for the best of the best

Still, no matter what I do

No matter what I tell myself

I can't break away from these fuck boys

These triffling, no good for nothing...fuck boys!

SEA OF TEARS

Last night I cried a sea of tears for you

Cuz every time I close my eyes

The only image I see is you

STILL...

Let's be honest

I'm broken

Bruised and fragile

Black and blue

From all the let downs

Yet still in need of love

PRINCE CHARMING

Oh, Prince Charming!

Where, oh where could you be?

I've searched high and low, far and wide

Endured scars and blisters

From this hell on earth

Just to discover that all the frogs I've kissed

Are all the same

No matter the shade, height or look

In a world of Jack'd and Grinder

This feat is surely impossible

Why can't I just meet a guy

Who can prove to be phenomenal?

I don't need perfection

Just give me protection

See I'm looking for affection

An undeniable connection

Someone to take me as I am

Despite my imperfections

Is it too much to ask for?

Is it really too much?

Should I simply throw the towel in

And call it another loss?

Cuz no one dates anymore

They're all really a bore

Eyes only set on the physical

It makes this shit so much more difficult

A MAN WHO WANTS TO BE KEPT

I should never have to chase you
Or beg for a moment of your busy day

I should never be sitting here all alone
With phone in hand
And not a single response from you

You should show me how much you care
Show me how badly you need me!

Because a man who truly wants to be kept
Will show how he feels through his actions
And not with the results of broken promises

A man who wants this as much as I do
Is gonna be right here by my side
Without me ever left to wonder

WHAT DJ REALLY NEEDS

I just need someone who's on my level

Not to sound arrogant

But I know I'm the shit

I'm far from perfect

But perfectly the best version of me

Can you match my flyness?

Not physically, but spiritually, mentally

On a level you've never seen before

Cuz you see, what DJ really needs

What I absolutely have to have

Is a grown ass man, ready for commitment

Not a lil' boy pretending to be something

He could never measure up to

*"You're a liability
I can't risk falling for"*

MISCOMMUNICATION

Miscommunication…

Caused our mouths to shout obscenities

We argued so much

We forgot what we were fighting for

I look to you and only feel regret

You stare back at me

Wishing you could forget

It began with stimulating phone conversations

Now I barely even get a text back

Breakups make us wiser

In time, it makes us a survivor

THE FEAR

We continuously drag our feet

Holding off on letting go

Afraid of moving on

All out of fear

We'll end up alone

Without a love

To call our own

LETTING GO AIN'T EASY

The longer I hold on
The harder this is gonna be
...for the both of us

I can't continue to hide from the truth
Masking the inevitable with a Band-Aid

It was my failed attempt
To protect your beautiful heart
I couldn't allow myself
To bruise that gentle soul

But here we are
Face to face
Body to body

And the love and affection
I once thought I had for you
Now has proven to be
Nothing more than a facade

We both searched high and low

For that perfect someone

Praying we'd find it within each other

Yet, how can that be our reality

When the truth persistently whispers in my ear

…This heart no longer skips a beat around you

TRUTHFULLY SPEAKING

Honestly, I can't allow myself

To love a stranger any longer

I take one look in your direction

And don't recall who you are

As the seasons changed

So have you, my darling

Now I stare into your eyes

Knowing damn well

Things will never be the same

IT IS WHAT IT IS

When you give and give

While receiving nothing in return

What else can you expect

But a tainted soul

And tears of regret?

IF I STAY

If I remain in your arms until morning

Would anything really change?

Would you do your absolute best

To heal every bruise?

Kiss away every tear?

CAREFUL WHAT U PRAY 4

I thought he was the blessing

I prayed night and day for

Until he plagued my life like a curse

DON'T WASTE UR TIME

Why give someone all of your energy?

Or even an ounce of your affection

When they can't even send a text back?

DRUNKEN REVELATIONS

These ho's don't have the capability to love

They reach out for you when they need it most

Then it's on to the next victim in line

The moment you let them inside

THESE SCARS

Love too hard

Give too much

And you'll be left

With third degree burns

Scarred for life

Marked by unsightly wounds

That will never heal

IS THERE ANY HOPE?

This generation doesn't know how to love

We acquire something new

Use it until we're exasperated

Toss it to the side like garbage

And then we resume this never-ending cycle

"He closed his eyes
As the silence surrounded him
With the anxiety diminishing
He allowed himself to do
The very thing he'd dreamed of all along
...He exhaled"

THAT SMALL VOICE INSIDE

You stepped onto the ledge

Vision cloudy

Palms sweaty

Wanted to end it all

Yet in the midst

Of all your suffering

The little voice

Inside your head

Reminded you this

Is not the end

God is far from finished

Working through you

So you closed your eyes

Took a deep breath

Exhaled

All while summoning up the courage

Not to take that leap

A LOVE LETTER 4 U

I just want you to know

I am so proud of you for living in your truth

Attempting to survive out here

Ain't the least bit easy

It never will be

And how could it

When society refuses once again

To make an effort in understanding us

And whenever we turn on the news

Yet another one of us

Is beaten, abused, and even worse

Murdered!

Surviving out here is a far cry

From a blissful walk in the park

Yet still...

We continue to march on

With our heads held high

And pride in loving who we are

We're all in this together

Whether we've been out and proud

For ten years or more

Or just recently discovering who we are

It doesn't matter if we identify as

GAY or LESBIAN

TRANS or NONBINARY

Because the truth of the matter is

Our unity makes us stronger than ever

With it, we possess all the power we'd ever need

To face whatever adversity may come our way

We can't stop because of how far we've come

And we won't stop

Because we have so much more to prove

I WISH

I wish I could sit you down

On an easy Sunday afternoon

Take you by the hand

And simply instruct you to

BREATHE!

Don't worry about tomorrow

Just continue living in the moment

Accept the things you cannot change

Be grateful for all the things you can

Don't neglect all your God-given talents

Because you fear others may judge

Life is too short to spend it

With doubts and lingering depression

Life is too precious to be afraid of sharing

Your ever-glowing light with the world!

Don't let it burn out!

I wish I could give all these lessons to you

Save you years of trouble

Navigating through life

And attempting to find yourself

But if we pressed rewind on the clock

And I told everything I felt you needed

Would you still possess that enduring

Strength that's deep within you now?

Would there be the slightest chance of you

Appreciating all the trials and tribulations?

Keep pushing forward

To everything you deserve in this world

For the marathon is never-ending

And your light is never diming!

THIS TIME AROUND...

This time around…

Don't feed me those false promises

Leading me on to believe

Once the deed is done, you'll remain in my bed

This time around…

Don't bother me with your bright ideas

Of hope and a better tomorrow

We both know you're only here for the moment

Soon to fade away like a ghost in the morning

This time around…

I've got absolutely no choice

But to remain true to my intuition

I'll listen to the wise head on my shoulders

Instead of the rebellious one within my pants

No doubt about it, I'll steer clear of the bullshit

No more taking three steps backward

When it should be ten steps forward

This time around…

I'll be wiser, smarter

And a much better version of me

I'll choose to put myself first

And carelessly cast your needs in the wind

For we both know I've always remained second

With not the slightest chance

Of ever obtaining your number one spot

This time around…

Oh yes, things will be different

I've found the sun in the mist of your darkness

I've awakened myself

From that once captivating spell

And now can see things as they truly are

I won't be needing you

Or anything that sparks a memory

I'm only in need of myself

It's me, myself, and I taking the world by storm

One day at a time

This time around...

YOU + ME

For all these months

All these days

It's for sure, without a shadow of a doubt

Been about you

And now for the remainder of my life

Without a single doubt in my mind

It's gonna be about me

All about me

You + me

Brings on the heartbreak

You + me

Brings out the worst of me

You + me

Should've never existed

THE DEVIL IS A LIE

If there ever comes a day in this life

When I must decide between

Loving you or loving me...

The devil is a lie if you ever thought

I'd choose you

THE GRASS AIN'T GREENER

He thought I was foolin' around

When I calmly warned

Him to get his shit together

He saw it as a joke

When I asked him to

Come retrieve his shit

Now I'm the one who's laughing

As he sits and reminisces

BLACK KING

Black King!
Black King!

You gotta quit playin' yourself

You know your worth and what you deserve
You know settling for less is absolutely absurd
You're aware of your own beauty
More than anyone else
So in what world does it make sense
To settle for less?

Why give those less than worthy
Another piece of you?
A piece of your heart?
A piece of your body?
A piece of your soul?

Wise up before you spend your days
Wasting your love on undeserving souls

When you could claim your crown

And all the while be loving yourself

THE BEAUTY OF SELF-LOVE

Find yourself a partner

Who appreciates the same beauty

You see when you gaze in the mirror

I NEED MORE

Sometimes we get so caught up in love

And simply the idea of falling in love

That we bypass what's most important

Like what does he bring to the table?

What can he do for you

That you can't already do for yourself?

Looks fade as we age

What on earth will remain

If the only thing he possesses is

Beauty and no brains?

THANK ME LATER

Know yourself

And in return

You will know your worth

HE WASN'T WORTH IT

No more tears

On your pillow

Throughout the night

No more wondering

Why he doesn't care

Or won't stand behind his word

No more crying

No more worry

No more deception

No more insecurities

No more...

LESSONS IN LOVE

Don't lose yourself

In the process of

Aiming to please him

THE STAGES OF LOVING U

Stage One

I cried like they would be no tomorrow

Stage Two

I dried my tears and regretted those 3 words

Stage Three

I promptly disposed of every trace

Of evidence that links me to you

Stage Four

I accepted you weren't the one

And I deserve far better

HOLD FAST

Hold fast young heart

Hold fast

Don't you know in the end

It's all gonna work out?

Hold fast young heart

Hold fast

You should know by now

This pain won't be forever

Hold fast young heart

Hold fast

You're one in a million

And Mr. Right is still out there waiting

SOMEDAY, ONE DAY

I'm sure of it

100 percent certain

That one of these days

I'm gonna stumble

Across the man of my dreams

He's out there

I have to believe

That day is bound to come

And I'll meet that being soon

The one who'll give me all the love I dish out

Right back in return

No questions asked

BACK 2 ME

I'm ready to let go
Of all the heartbreak
And ghastly memories

Ready to start over
Loving myself
And finding happy

DAY BY DAY

I'm healing and learning

Always evolving

Not quite who I wanna be

But striving every day towards

Who I should be

CROSSROADS

When you find yourself

Losing your way

At the dead end

Of a crossroad

Fall onto bended knees

And simply choose

Whatever brings you peace

OH MOTHER!

Where on God's green earth

Would I be without my dearest mother?

My first love

And the one being who'll still have love for me

Even in my darkest hour

The one person who's been there from the start

And won't leave my side as others come and go

If I lose my balance

And can't fathom a reason to get up

If I suddenly feel this journey of life

Is too difficult to carry on

You remain behind me

Standing brave and tall

Helping me climb that mountain

And erasing any fears of failure

I praise the good Lord above

And sing to the highest mountain

Thanking God for such a blessing

For no one could ever compare

No one could ever replace

And nothing could ever erase

The love for the woman I call mother

R.I.P.

Last night I dreamed about you
You were alive and well
Back from the dead
With your heart beating stronger than ever

You sat me upon your lap
Calmly told me about your day
And although it was only a dream
It felt as surreal as ever

Why did I have to wake up?
Because in a perfect world you'd be here
Here to comfort mom's breaking heart
And here to walk amongst the living

But Heaven saw fit to grant you wings
And now there's no more pain, no more hurting
No more coughing, no more wheezing
Now you can rest easy
And fly amongst the angels

Until we meet again

THE GREATEST LOVE

I searched for love in toads
Who never became my Prince Charming
I gave one hundred and ten percent
When I knew I'd never get back half
I sightlessly chased after all those men
Hoping for a chance at true love

But all the time
There has been a guiding light
Trailing behind my every move
Still with me after every mishap
And wrong turn
It's always guided me back to the light

I've had this love all along
It's remained in the background
Fighting against the darkness
Claiming victory in the battle
Of who wins my soul

I was too blinded by the world to notice

But no matter where I may go

And what I may do

This love from up above

Will always remain…

The greatest love of all

AND HE ALWAYS WILL

The good Lord is always with us

Even when we sink to our lowest

Even when we've done the unthinkable

And don't deserve a second chance

He's still there

Loving us

Protecting us

Leading us

…And He always will

AND HE ALWAYS WILL PT. 2

The good Lord is with me

Even when I'm at my lowest

With my head bowed in the midst of failure

And back up against the wall

AND HE ALWAYS WILL PT. 3

I can see the light

At the end of the tunnel

I can sense God's love

All around me

Protecting me from the evil

That taunts my soul to stray

GOD'S WORKING IT OUT

I don't know the time or place

I don't know when or how

But one thing I do know for sure is…

God's got something magnificent coming to me

I may have gone through hell and back

And I may not be where I wanna be in life

But one thing I can never doubt is…

God's forever working in my favor

WE GOT THIS

Why do we doubt ourselves
When we know God is in control?

We are well aware
He's guiding our steps
Holding our hand
Leading us to our destiny

Yet we allow the world to cripple and blind us
Into believing we are not good enough
What's worse is we fall victim to believe
If it's not happening now, it never will

We compare ourselves and our situations
To celebrities on social media
When our focus should be centered
Fully on creating our own path

Trust God
And his timing

Let us never forget

We got this!

Printed in Great Britain
by Amazon